THE BOOK OF TAYLOR

THE BOOK OF TAYLOR

THE BOOK OF TAYLOR

THE BOOK OF TAYLOR

THE BOOK OF

50 reasons Taylor Swift rules the world

TAYLOR

THE BOOK OF

TAYLOR

Smith Street Books

BILLIE OLIVER AND STEPHANIE SPARTELS

Taylor entered this ever-grateful world on DECEMBER 13, 1989, meaning her star sign is SAGITTARIUS. Pretty unsurprising, really.

Taylor's early years were spent on her family's **CHRISTMAS TREE FARM.** Rural life wasn't exactly merry year-round though...

Taylor's grandma Marjorie was an **OPERA**

SINGER

and TV personality.

Taylor has often pointed to Marjorie's creativity and hustle as a source of major inspiration.

The first three chords Taylor learned on guitar came from an unlikely mentor: a computer repairman visiting the family home when she was 12...

Taylor is a proud cat girly. Her two Scottish Folds are named MEREDITH GREY and OLIVIA BENSON, after the iconic characters from GREY'S ANATOMY and LAW & ORDER: SVU,

while her Ragdoll is called **BENJAMIN BUTTON.** As in: **BRAD PITT** and the curious case of.

Ain't nobody messing with Taylor's clique. Her list of besties reads like a pop cultural fever dream:

Selena Gomez, Gigi Hadid, Blake Lively, Cara Delevingne and the HAIM sisters.

If an object can be forced to make a tune, Taylor can play it.

She's an accomplished **ACOUSTIC** and **ELECTRIC GUITARIST, PIANIST, UKULELE-IST** and **BANJO-IST.**

Those NBA fans unknowingly lucked out with some of the cheapest Tay-Tay tickets on record.

SHANiA TWAIN, the OG empress of country-pop, is Taylor's most important musical influence.

Taylor has also said she'll forever be indebted to the pop path forged by **BRITNEY SPEARS.**

In 2009, Taylor shattered

COUNTRY MUSIC RECORDS,

racking up more digital downloads than any other country artist in history.

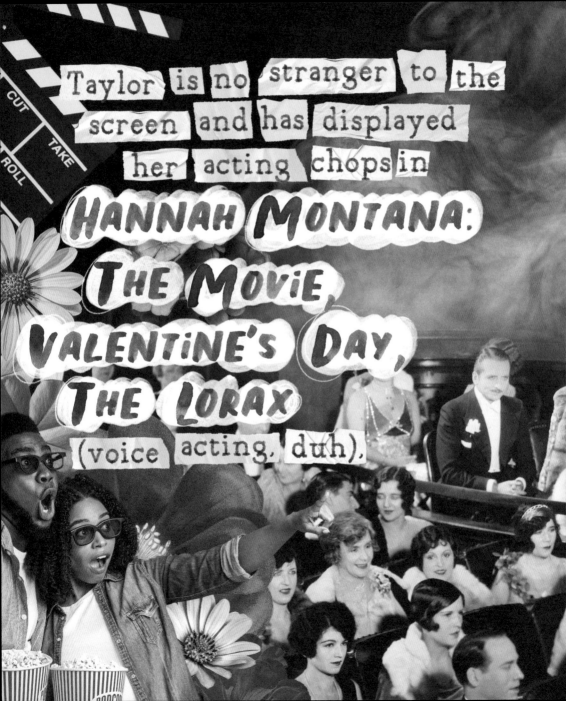

Taylor is no stranger to the screen and has displayed her acting chops in

Hannah Montana: The Movie, Valentine's Day, The Lorax (voice acting, duh).

Cats and Amsterdam, as well as episodes of CSI and New Girl.

At the 2018 **AMERICAN MUSIC AWARDS,** Taylor added yet another record to the history books, becoming the most-decorated female AMA winner of all time,

and knocking **WHiTNEY HOUSTON** out of the top spot.

Taylor was first "discovered" in 2005, at Nashville's **BLUEBIRD CAFE** where her heartfelt sound piqued the interest of **BIG MACHINE RECORDS.**

PRINCE WILLIAM once sang "LIVIN' ON A PRAYER" with TAYLOR and BON JOVI at a charity event.

We hope his Royal Highness was ever grateful to share the stage with a queen of Taylor's stature.

Taylor Swift has been crowned Billboard's **WOMAN OF THE YEAR** twice (so far), and in 2019 she became their inaugural **WOMAN OF THE DECADE.**

At age 14, Taylor wrote *A Girl Named Girl*, a 350-page novel which has never been published. We wait with bated breath.

13 has a special place in Taylor's heart. In her words... "**I WAS BORN ON THE 13TH. I TURNED 13 ON FRIDAY THE 13TH. MY FIRST ALBUM WENT GOLD IN 13 WEEKS. MY FIRST NO.1 SONG HAD A 13-SECOND INTRO ..."**

And the
coincidences
don't stop
there.

Once, SWiFT 89 invited of her biggest fans over to her house for a listening party.

Ever the hostess with the most-est, **TAYLOR** baked fresh **COOKiES** for all her guests. No biggie.

Taylor is the first artist in **HISTORY** to have six separate albums sell more than **ONE MILLION COPIES** in their first week of release. Talk about overachieving.

It turns out Taylor was a co-writer of the RIHANNA and CALVIN HARRIS hit "THIS IS WHAT YOU CAME FOR."

Taylor used the pen name **Nils Sjoberg** and has hinted that there are other undercover aliases she's used to **GHOSTWRITE** bangers over the years.

Academic overachievers no longer need to aim for the **LOFTY FiELDS** of medicine or law.

because you can now study **TAYLOR SWIFT** at the **CLIVE DAVIS INSTITUTE** in New York.

In 2012, Taylor's hit "WE ARE NEVER GETTING BACK TOGETHER" became the fastest-selling digital single of all time, sending the Swiftie group chats into overdrive.

Taylor made GRAMMY history after MIDNIGHTS became her fourth album to take out ALBUM OF

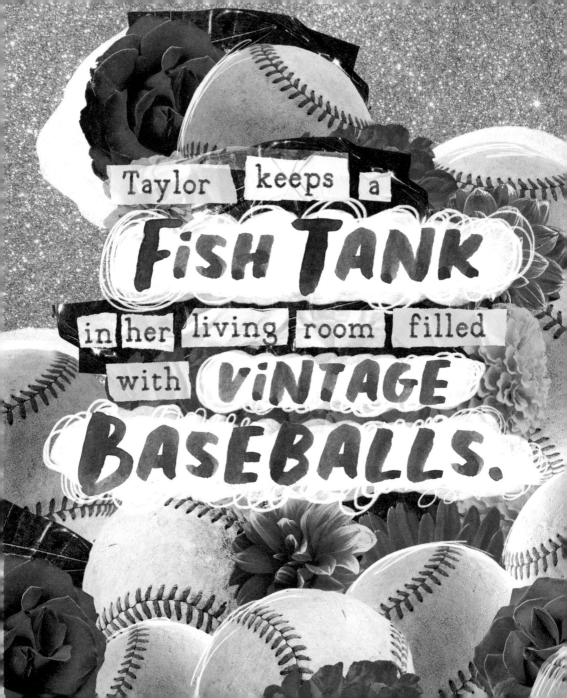

Taylor keeps a **Fish Tank** in her living room filled with **VINTAGE BASEBALLS.**

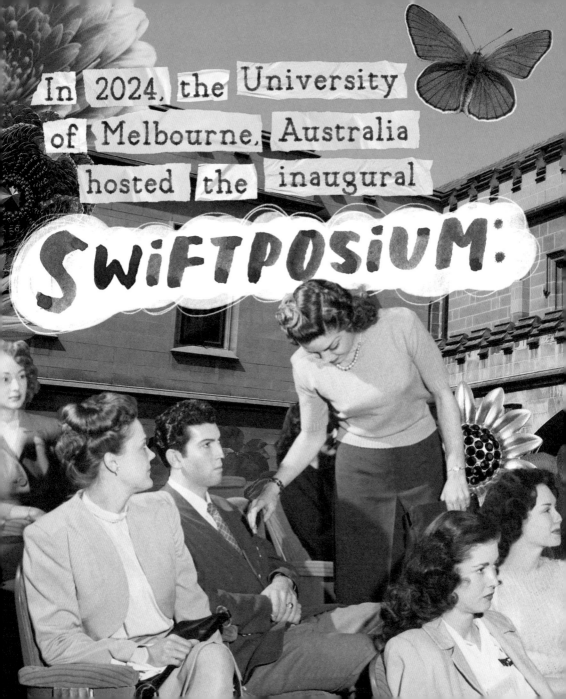

In 2024, the University of Melbourne, Australia hosted the inaugural

SWIFTPOSIUM:

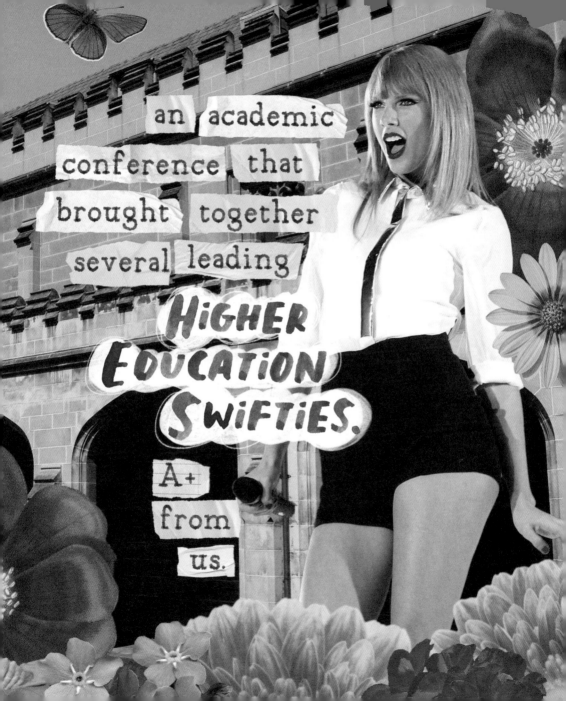

an academic conference that brought together several leading

HiGHER EDUCATioN SwiFTiES.

A+ from us.

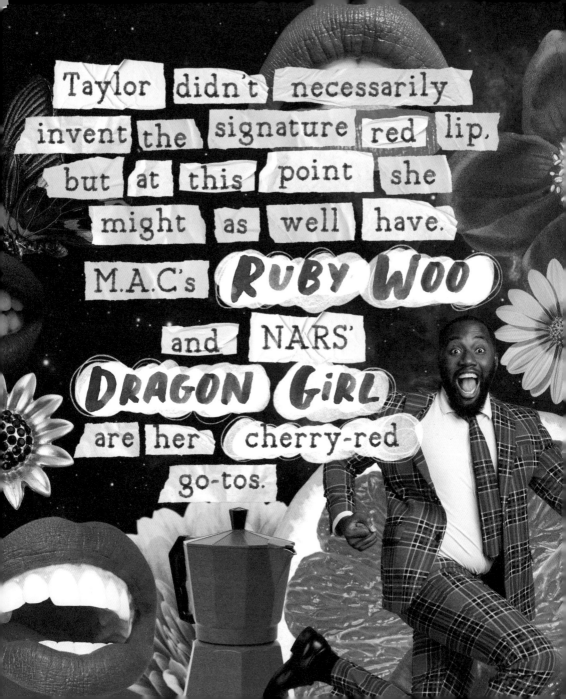

Taylor didn't necessarily invent the signature red lip, but at this point she might as well have. M.A.C's *Ruby Woo* and NARS' *Dragon Girl* are her cherry-red go-tos.

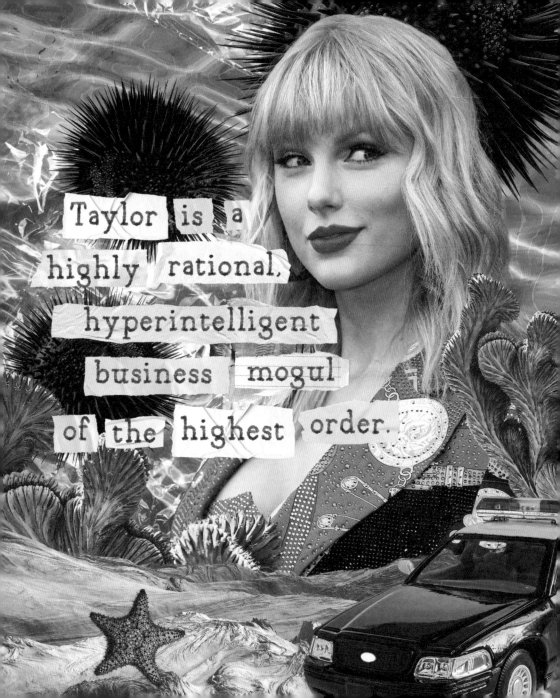

Taylor is a highly rational, hyperintelligent business mogul of the highest order.

Taylor broke the internet for the umpteenth time when she was spotted by a fan eating a piece of chicken with ketchup and **SEEMINGLY RANCH.**

Heinz didn't skip a beat, dropping a limited edition **KETCHUP AND SEEMINGLY RANCH** within 48 hours.

At 19, **TAYLOR SWIFT** hosted SNL and gave us a rare treat by writing her own opening monologue — which she of course sung. Naturally, it was a slay.

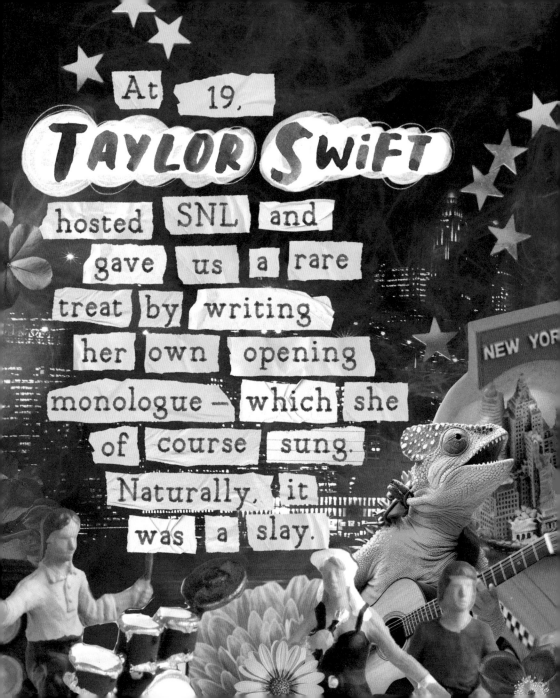

JACK ANTONOFF

is one of Taylor's long-time collaborators and producers, and works with an impressive posse of pop icons including **LANA DEL RAY LORDE, FKA TWIGS,** and **TROYE SIVAN.**

Swift donned a director's cap for her first short film

ALL TOO WELL,

starring

Sadie Sink
and Dylan
O'Brien.

In the not-too-distant future, Taylor will make her feature directorial **DEBUT** with an **ORIGINAL SCRIPT** from hers truly.

Dare we say one step closer to Taylor reaching EGOT status ...

Taylor's Eras Tour quite literally **BROKE THE iNTERNET.** Ticket sites went into full meltdown and millions of Swifties came close to rioting.

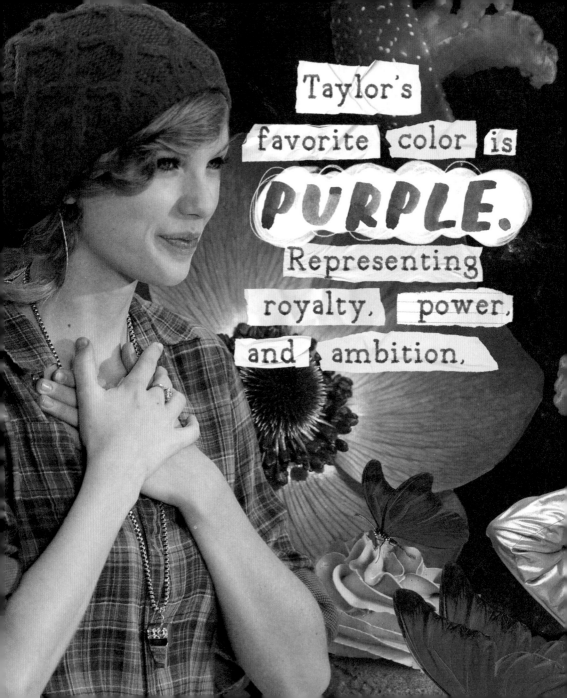

Taylor's favorite color is **PURPLE.** Representing royalty, power, and ambition,

purple really does seem like the most Taylor color of them all.

While writing **EVERMORE** during the pandemic, Taylor has said she was watching Ang Lee's 1995 adaptation of **SENSE AND SENSIBILITY** on repeat as inspiration.

It makes perfect sense, really.

"Kiss Me" by Sixpence None the Richer was the first song Taylor ever learned to play on the guitar.

The world needs Taylor's studio cover of that track.

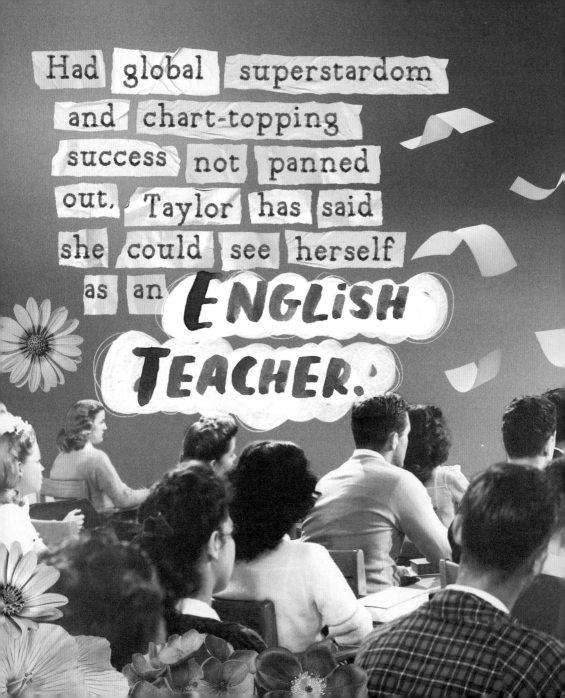

Had global superstardom and chart-topping success not panned out, Taylor has said she could see herself as an **ENGLISH TEACHER.**

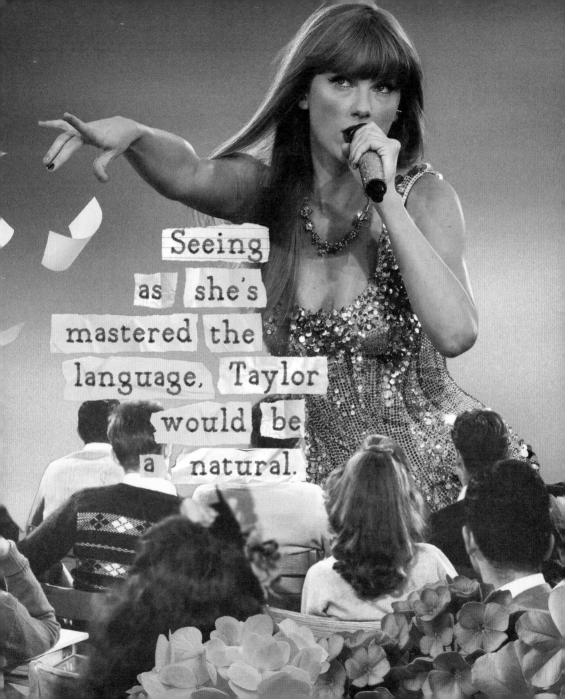

Seeing as she's mastered the language, Taylor would be a natural.

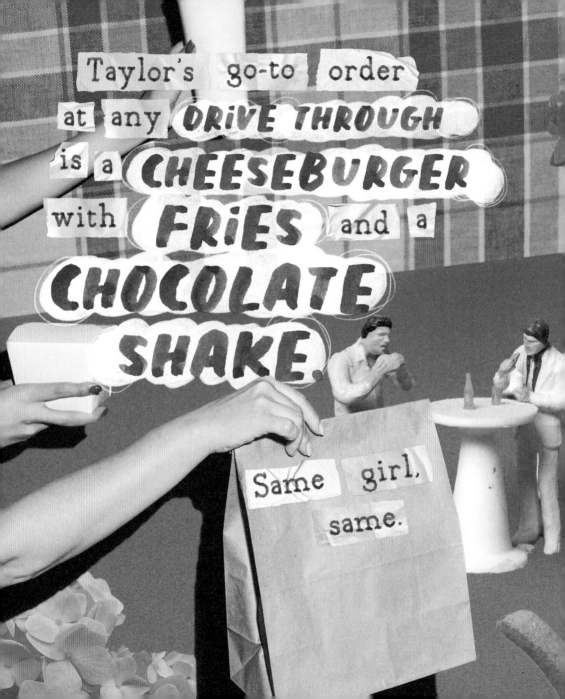

Like so many of us mere mortals, Taylor's favorite TV show is FRIENDS.

The iconic 1990s sitcom has garnered fans over multiple generations, just like Taylor's own legion of fans.

For as long as she can remember, Taylor's favorite film has been LOVE ACTUALLY.

To bring everything full circle, she starred in **VALENTINE'S DAY** - the film's spiritual successor.

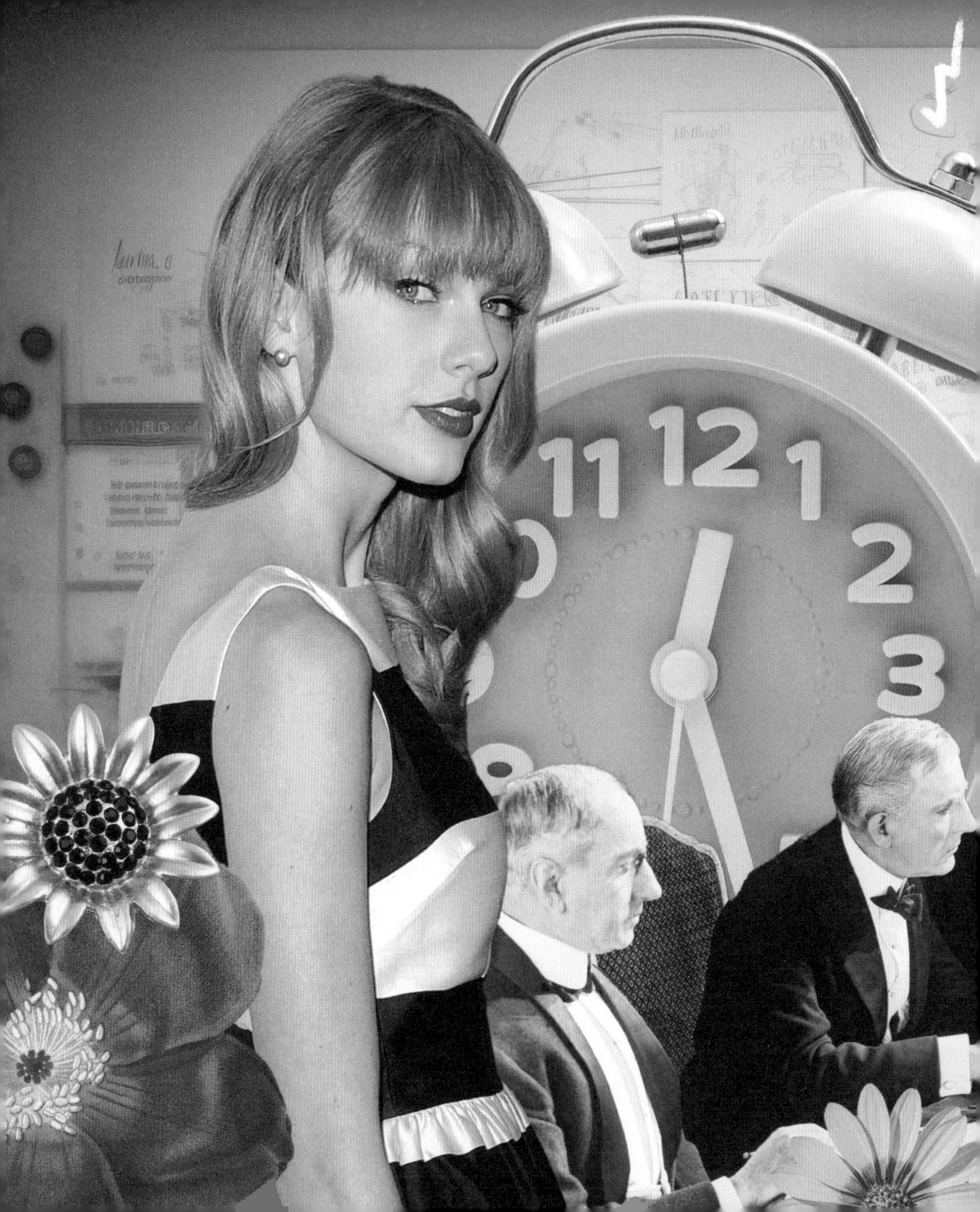

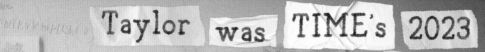

Taylor was TIME's 2023

PERSON OF THE YEAR.

It's about time they caught up to what the rest of us have known for years.

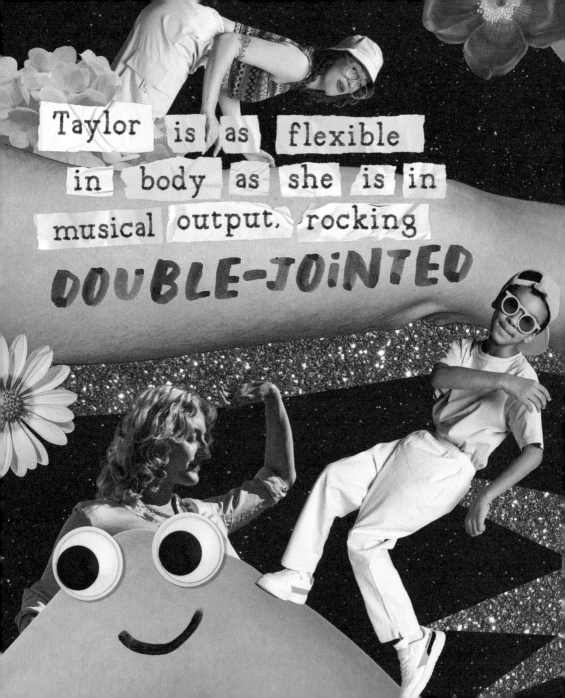

Taylor is as flexible in body as she is in musical output, rocking **DOUBLE-JOINTED**

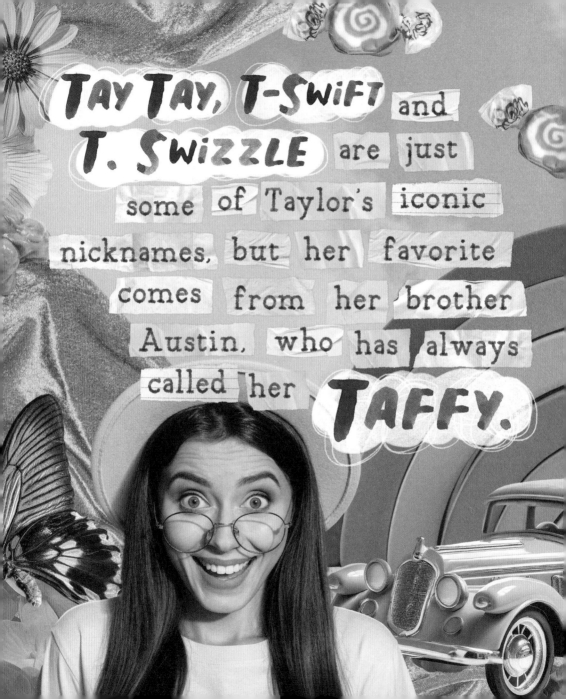

TAY TAY, T-SWIFT and **T. SWIZZLE** are just some of Taylor's iconic nicknames, but her favorite comes from her brother Austin, who has always called her **TAFFY.**

Probably because she's as sweet as can be.

Never fatiguing from her role as a

GLOBAL MEGASTAR,

Taylor has said that she will stop any fan on the street wearing Taylor Swift merch to say

Taylor feels an innate (and wholesome) connection to **DOLPHINS.** I'm sure any dolphin would love Taylor to join their pod.

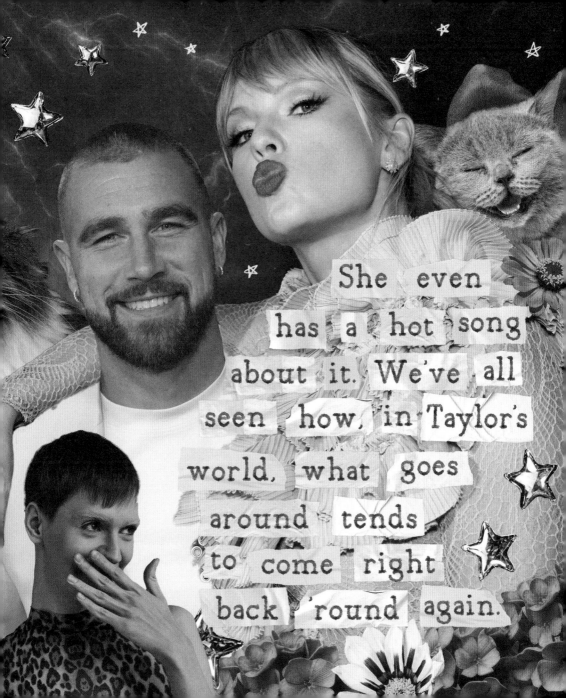

She even has a hot song about it. We've all seen how, in Taylor's world, what goes around tends to come right back 'round again.

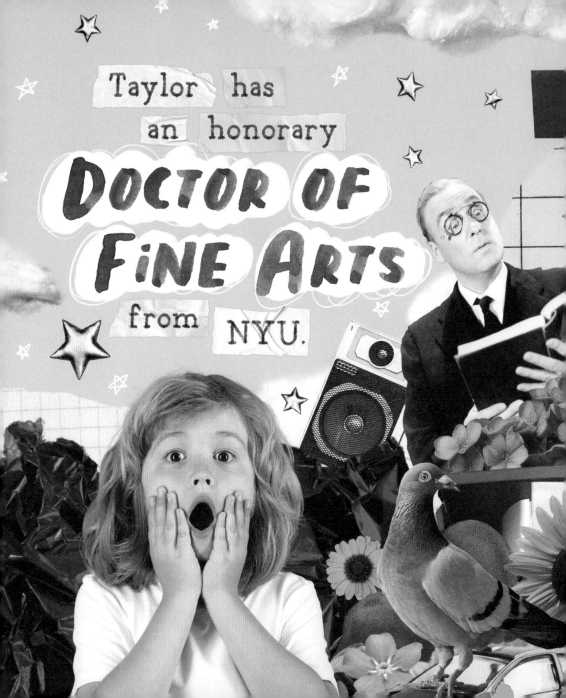

Taylor is known by her nearest and dearest as the

QUEEN OF BREAKFAST

(with omelets as her specialty).

Taylor is a fierce advocate for artists' rights over their own music and intellectual property. And lucky for us, because otherwise we wouldn't have

TAYLOR'S VERSION!

Published in 2024 by Smith Street Books
Naarm (Melbourne) | Australia
smithstreetbooks.com

ISBN: 978-192304-949-9

Smith Street Books respectfully acknowledges the Wurundjeri People of the Kulin Nation, who are the Traditional Owners of the land on which we work, and we pay our respects to their Elders past and present.

Cover photograph © PA Images / Alamy Stock Photo
Copyright stock photography © alamy.com, gettyimages.com.au, shutterstock.com, stock.adobe.com and unsplash.com

Publisher: Paul McNally
Project editor: Lucy Grant
Design and layout: Stephanie Spartels

Printed & bound in China by C&C Offset Printing Co., Ltd.

Book 333

10 9 8 7 6 5 4 3 2 1

Please note: This title is not affiliated with or endorsed in any way by Taylor. We are just big fans. Please don't sue us.

MIX
Paper | Supporting responsible forestry
FSC® C008047
FSC
www.fsc.org

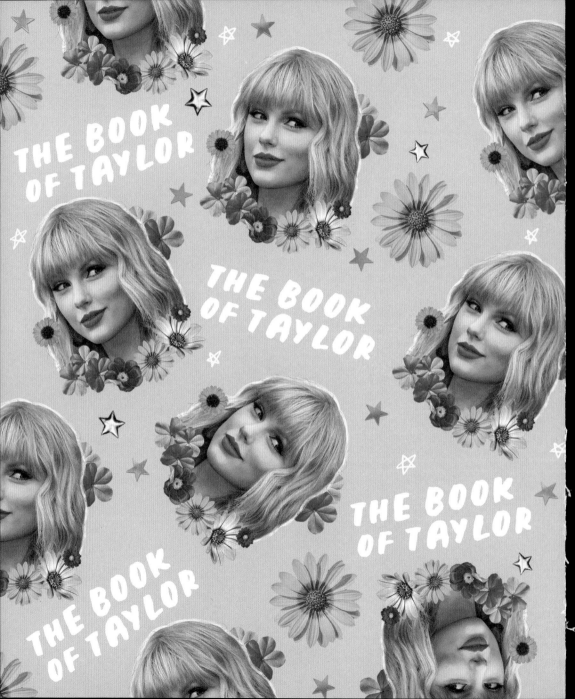